The Way We Live

ALSO BY BURT KIMMELMAN

POETRY

*As If Free* (2009)
*There Are Words* (2007)
*Somehow* (2005)
*The Pond at Cape May Point* (2002), paintings by Fred Caruso
*First Life* (2000)
*Musaics* (1992)

CRITICISM

*The "Winter Mind": William Bronk and American Letters*
    (1998)
*The Poetics of Authorship in the Later Middle Ages:*
    *The Emergence of the Modern Literary Persona* (1996)
*The Facts on File Companion to American Poetry*
    (2007, Co-Editor)
*The Facts on File Companion to 20th-Century American*
    *Poetry* (2005, Editor)

*The Way We Live*

Poems

by

BURT KIMMELMAN

2011
DOS MADRES PRESS

# DOS MADRES PRESS INC.
P.O.Box 294, Loveland, Ohio 45140
www.dosmadres.com    editor@dosmadres.com

Dos Madres is dedicated to the belief that the small press is essential to the vitality of contemporary literature as a carrier of the new voice, as well as the older, sometimes forgotten voices of the past. And in an ever more virtual world, to the creation of fine books pleasing to the eye and hand.

Dos Madres is named in honor of Vera Murphy and Libbie Hughes, the "Dos Madres" whose contributions have made this press possible.

Dos Madres Press, Inc. is an Ohio Not For Profit Corporation and a 501 (c) (3) qualified public charity. Contributions are tax deductible.

Executive Editor: Robert J. Murphy

Book Design: Elizabeth H. Murphy
www.illusionstudios.net
Typset in Adobe Garamond Pro & Dali

ACKNOWLEDGMENTS
Some of these poems have appeared, at times in earlier versions, in *Big Scream, EOAGH, Golden Handcuffs Review, Little Red Leaves, The Newark Review, Talisman: A Journal of Contemporary Poetry and Poetics,* and *Tuesday; An Art Project.*
Author Photo: Diane Simmons

ISBN 978-1-933675-64-0

*For Diane and Jane, as always*

# Table of Contents

The Way We Live

# Jane Planting Flowers

Spring 2010

She tilts her head to view
the white impatiens she
holds in her hand, the light
of the afternoon caught
in them — thinking where they

belong among blue and
yellow petals on their
stems newly rooted in
black loam. She has come home
as if to arrange our

garden this spring — having
left her stray-dog artist's
life in the city, for
a time, its car alarms,
gritty sidewalks and shared

apartments. I say how
lovely the backyard looks
and will not let on her
sitting there, at the edge
of the grass, is what I

mean — this sunny day, in
the shade of our maple
tree from which she used to
swing, years ago, until
it was too dark to see.

# Marlene Dumas' The Kiss, 2003

Museum of Modern Art, New York City, 2009

What might not be dreamt
in the stupor of
Saturday night by
herself — she lies face
down against the white

sheets on her bed, the
dark line of her sealed
eyelids, her lips just
barely apart that
had once said his name.

# Late January Morning

I step out the door on this
somber, cold January
morning to get the daily
newspaper tossed onto my
lawn covered snow white though it
is still before dawn, and as

I bend down I hear a bird
on a distant bare branch of
a tree singing a song I
have last heard when there were leaves
everywhere I looked — a call
to meet, to feather the nest —

so what could it mean in these
dark days? Perhaps, as I have
done, simply contemplating
a moment in my modest
domestic life, this bird has
foolishly, proudly proclaimed

it has a home — no need to
fly south — against the stark chill,
tempting the fates, and knowing,
more than I, who will migrate
to my kitchen for some tea,
the nights are getting shorter.

# Alhambra Steps

Leaving the palace
we descend the steep
stone stairs arm in arm —
you pulling me down,
me holding you up.

# Mikvah* Warsaw Ghetto 1941

*At a screening of* A Film Unfinished, *New York City 2010*

They wade into the
water, naked, in
silence, shoulders hunched
over, in their fear
betraying the lens.

There are dark splotches
in the celluloid
where their groins were and
where the soldiers, out
of the frame, could aim.

In far off Berlin
an information
officer realized
what he was seeing,
hid it in a vault.

A young girl in the
ghetto who, by luck,
has become an old
woman, is being
shown the restored film.

Watching the haggard
bodies, the clumsy
attempts to obey,
she sighs, as if she
has to be polite.

"When the Germans showed
up there was always
trouble," she says, the
fact of the matter
unalterable.

# Big Storm

Beneath the eave
the birdfeeder
swinging in swirls
of driven snow —

bluejays, sparrows
and cardinals
gather as if
a single flock,

in the white air
flying to the
hoard of seeds, its
scarce sustenance —

blue, brown and red
birds daring each
other for a
tenuous perch.

# With Fred Caruso, Standing in Front of Pierre Bonnard's Corner of the Dining Room at Le Cannet

"The Late Interiors," Metropolitan Museum of Art,
New York City, 27 March 2009

Nothing much ever happens, yet there
is a comfort in simply living
among the objects of the day — bowls
of fruit, a vase of flowers on a
red tablecloth holding light coming
from a window outside of the frame.

Her face is turned sideways above her
bright yellow shawl as she looks for what
she has meant to take with her, leaving
the room — or is she, in a backward
glance at the urn on the mantelpiece,
admiring her arrangements of things?

Fred and I stand talking, the painting
of the dining room behind him, and
I think about Bonnard's soft tones, then
about Fred's portrayals in their hot
colors, his people — young and full with
desire, and smiling at the viewer.

In Bonnard's picture we slowly come
to notice a faint longing in the
day itself — the woman's dissolving
thought, what she wants still remaining, like
the scene before us, which is not quite
real but true enough for the moment.

# On a Terrace, Waiting to Enter El Palacio Nazaries, Alhambra

A man reads
of the old
palace out
loud from his
French brochure.

His wife stares
across the
valley to
the mountains
in their snow.

# Cicadas, Mid July

How odd the occasion, the whirring
of the cicadas, surprising once
we start to hear their secret business,
unseen no matter where we look — we
pause in our morning talk, wondering
when they arrived and why the summer's
unforgiving heat begins with their
advent and later the cool early
evenings settle in with their silence.

Spring, in its false starts with the pushing
through soil and snow of its first flowers,
their small shocks of color, held us in
blossoms and leaves so in a while we
let go of the thought that the light and
warmth would ever come to an end, but
the cicadas do their work — no more
twitters of birds, our regret spun in
the din and the waning of the light.

# Stone Love

Metropolitan Museum of Art, New York City, 15 May 2011
*for Jayne Holsinger and Hugh Seidman*

The round torsos
hide the stone for
a moment — the
idea there

of bodies pressed
together, their
resilient flesh
in form itself.

Later a young
couple, arm in
arm, passes me
on the street, lost

in the warm spring
day — the fact of
love, our belief
in it, its touch.

# Thanksgiving Morning

Yellow flowers leaning from
a glass vase of water on

a wooden table where a

petal has fallen — autumn
sun, a wayward guest, shines through.

# Summer, Young Woman by the Westside Drive

She walks along the
river, one hand to
her ear, talking with
her telephone in
the afternoon sun.

The cars and trucks on
the drive pass her by,
speeding the other
way, their small breezes
easing the vast heat.

She trails her other
hand behind, fingers
brushing the hedge tops
planted beside the
way, their dried spring buds.

Her black dress, swirling
with each step, her bare
brown shoulders, arms and
legs gather in the
unforgiving light.

# The Way We Live

The hole dug, a few words spoken, we
are invited to cast the unearthed
soil upon the coffin below,
its skillfully carved six-pointed star.

His two sons, from among us, take up
the shovel in turn, and then his wife,
sobbing, then the rest of us, stepping
to the edge, back to the gathering.

Someone remembers the ritual
flag but it is too late to drape it
over him, the younger son saying,
helpfully, "it will be a keepsake."

The rabbi, in English, rehearses
this man's life, his generosity
and laughter, how resourceful he was,
the good husband and father he was.

Named *Pesach*,* which became Paul, he spent
his first Passover away from home
on a troop ship in the Pacific,
about to land on Guadalcanal.

The rabbi tells us of the unique
kindness we perform in attending
a funeral, a *mitzvah*** the dead
do not know, which they cannot repay.

At last the sons intone the *Kaddish*, ***
the older, his voice broken, convulsed
in sorrow, the Hebrew he studied
long ago alive for the first time.

* Hebrew and Yiddish for Passover
** A good deed
*** Jewish prayer used to mourn the death of a close relative

# Wild Onions (After Robert's Letter)

For Robert and Elizabeth Murphy

I think if I were very old I
would want the wild onions growing in
my yard to take up housekeeping with
me — "their flower heads," once "bobbing
in the wind," poking from a jar as
they fade to a fine dust, so I might
see in them who I have become — more
lovely than I am in the morning
mirror where I glimpse who I once was.

# The Deception

*Still Life* by Giorgio Morandi, 1955
Metropolitan Museum of Art, New York City, 2008

How easily we settle
into the picture — some squat,
plain boxes and a long-necked
bottle — those simple objects
arranged together so he
might catch them in their soft browns
and yellows, and among them
an intransigent, opaque
white spot, but everywhere else
in the canvas black traces
he must have applied with the
most informal of brush strokes.

He means to discomfit us
yet we surrender ourselves
to these sure shapes assembled
as for a camera though
without occasion, nothing
to be done, since it is best,
he must have thought, once he knew
he loved to paint, to leave things
unspoken — the mute smears of
color, the bare ground of the
horizontal — a made world,
something of his stubborn craft.

# Robin, Spring

The robin, claws hidden in
tall grass, hops forward and sings
a solitary note, hops
once more, stopping to sing two
notes, which loop through the air, then
tilts its head to eye the ground,
flies off to a nearby tree.

# Late November
## in the South Mountain Reservation

The day has taken on a plan
in the brief warmth of a late fall
sun, so Diane and I start our
walk through the bare trees, having left
the car in a drift of wet red
leaves by the road — no deer, no bird
either, but the stone bridge ahead,
and beyond it the waterfalls.

We climb alongside the cold spray
to reach the stream above, soft spot
of the mountain where it might yield
to us, where we sit and pour tea
from a thermos, sipping it out
of paper cups, and I think of
the *chanoyu* ceremony,*
as we watch the light on wet rocks.

*Japanese tea ceremony otherwise known as the *Way of Tea*, which involves the ritual preparation and presentation of particularly green tea.

## Domestic

Cutting board, knife, bread
crumbs in dawn light — she
stood and ate beside
the kitchen sink, then
got back into bed.

# At a Willem de Kooning Show with Michael Heller

Pace Gallery on Fifty-Seventh Street, New York City, May 2011

*Not a declaration which is truth*
*But a thing*
*Which is. It is the business of the poet*
*"To suffer the things of the world*
*And to speak them and himself out."*

        - George Oppen


Broad swirling brush strokes crossing
the canvas, their edges fade
in thinned-out paint and Mike talks
about how the bright yellow
leaks out of the light blue laid
on slightly thicker while I,
from over his shoulder, try

seeing what he sees — twisted
figures the colors make most
of all, what the artist saw
as his quandary, since what else
might have been the point? We drop
back onto the street and look
into the drizzle before

stepping on, the wild spring
among tall buildings that sound
the buses, trucks, taxicabs
bellying along the wet
swath of dark asphalt in their
commerce — not unlike, really,
"the business of the poet."

# Storm, Beach, Gull

Belmar, New Jersey, August 2009

Spatters of rain in the wind hurrying us
along the boardwalk, its evenly laid planks
of wood, unlike the wild day, repeating
themselves on toward a low-lying roof in
the gray distance, the slate water covers and
uncovers the darkened beach where birds leap up
and settle again, picking at what they can.

A white gull tries to tear apart the neck and
breast of a small dead bird found in the sand, the
limp body flopping about in its great beak,
but then lets go and rises in the air,
heavy wings fully spread in the droplets of
storm, slowly flapping, the mute ocean
gathering up the carcass in its embrace.

# Looking through the Picture Window at Poets House

Late March 2011, New York City

The filigree of twigs on bare
branches though the park, the river
beyond invisible in fog,
a woman pushes her baby
carriage along the street, holding
the hand of her older child,
a girl in red jacket and cap
prancing behind, looking away.

# Early April Morning

*dazed spring approaches*
- William Carlos Williams

A few birds twirling their notes in
the new light and my neighbor, hunched
over his garden, the hood of
his sweatshirt keeping his thoughts
to himself, looks past me as I bend
to take hold of the newspaper
tossed on my walk before dawn when
wet, dense darkness was all there was —

but then I hear his "good morning,"
he and I standing upright for
a moment before his turn back
to work, the bamboo prongs of his
rake softly scraping the soil
the night's rain has softened, to make
ready for planting flowers, the
early hour otherwise still.

# Arctic Terns

*White clouds like kerchiefs at parting*
*Are waved by the wandering wind,*
*And the heart of the wind*
*Aches at the silence of love.*
    - Pablo Neruda


Arctic terns touch down from the sky
every few years, leaving their life
of flight to raise their young and then,
in the waning light, lift off the
firm earth of Greenland to make their

way south — roving high above the
ocean, not too close to land but
looping east to trace the coast of
Africa or west along the
shores of South America, then

finally crossing the open
sea to the farthest reach of ice —
for a second season of days.
In large flocks they cye the water
for food, and once a male has fed

his future mate her fill of fish —
in a rite beyond gravity —
they join for their entire lives.
Yet flying must be an act of
solitude, an unfed longing.

BURT KIMMELMAN has published six previous collections of poetry – *As If Free* (Talisman House, Publishers, 2009), *There Are Words* (Dos Madres Press, 2007), *Somehow* (Marsh Hawk Press, 2005), *The Pond at Cape May Point* (Marsh Hawk Press, 2002), a collaboration with the painter Fred Caruso, *First Life* (Jensen/Daniels Publishing, 2000), and *Musaics* (Sputyen Duyvil Press, 1992). A poem from his newest book was featured on NPR's The Writer's Almanac. For over a decade he was Senior Editor of the now defunct *Poetry New York: A Journal of Poetry and Translation*. He is a professor of English at New Jersey Institute of Technology and the author of two book-length literary studies: *The "Winter Mind": William Bronk and American Letters* (Fairleigh Dickinson University Press, 1998); and, *The Poetics of Authorship in the Later Middle Ages: The Emergence of the Modern Literary Persona* (Peter Lang Publishing, 1996; paperback 1999). He also edited *The Facts on File Companion to 20th-Century American Poetry* (Facts on File, 2005) and co-edited T*he Facts on File Companion to American Poetry* (Facts on File, 2007). He has published scores of essays on medieval, modern, and contemporary poetry. A recent interview with Tom Fink appeared online in *Jacket 40*.

Visit BurtKimmelman.com
for further details and links.